What's In It for Me?

Getting the Most Out of Your Job

Greg Olsen

Published by
Innovative Management Solutions, LLC

Copyright © 2021 by Gregory K. Olsen. All rights reserved except as permitted under the United States Copyright Act of 1976. No part of this publication may be reproduced or distributed in any form or by any means, or stored in a data base or retrieval system, without prior written permission of the publisher and the author.

FIRST EDITION

ISBN: 978-1-7343331-5-2

This publication is designed to provide accurate and authoritative information in regard to the subject matter covered. It is sold with the understanding that the publisher is not engaged in rendering legal, accounting, or other professional service. If legal advice or other assistance is required, the services of a competent professional person should be sought.

This book is dedicated to all the wonderful people with whom I've had the pleasure to work over the years. I thank you for all you've taught me. Also, to my loving family who tolerated and supported me while I was learning.

Table of Contents

Chapter 1: Introduction

It's rather interesting that, as humans, we tend to look at everything from the viewpoint of "What's in it for me?" Some would associate that with selfishness. I look at it as a component of survival. When something new comes along, the only way we know how to deal with it is by determining what affect it might have on us. When change occurs, it's difficult to determine how that change will affect others. We don't know their thoughts, their fears, their desires or their inspiration, but we know those things about ourselves. It's not only common for these words to be the first thought that goes through our heads when something new happens, but also probably efficient for, in our relentless pursuit of survival, we need to ascertain how this change will affect us.

When faced with change at work, we need to evaluate how that change will affect us so we can determine how to react. Sometimes change is good and sometimes change isn't that easy to accept. How we respond to change will make a difference and our response will result in consequences, good or bad. This book, however, is not about how to address change, but rather about making changes in your life because you see the value of what's in it for you. It's about changes you choose to make that will make your job, and ultimately your life, better. For that reason, the subtitle is Getting the Most Out of Your Job.

That phrase, Getting the Most Out of Your Job, may have left you curious. You're fairly satisfied with your job. You're getting a paycheck and some benefits. You like most of the people you work with. The hours aren't too bad. It's a hassle once in a while, but for the most part, you can live with it. It's a job and you're glad to have one. So, aren't you already getting the most out of your job?

Perhaps you are, but are opportunities and promotions coming your way frequently? Are you receiving appropriate wages, not just competitive wages for the work you do? Are bonuses plentiful? Is your career climbing fast? If you answered no to any of these questions and aren't currently getting everything out of your job that YOU want, then I encourage you to read this book.

The path to satisfaction in your job involves two components: 1) Maximizing your relationships with others and 2) Becoming the best you can be. Utilizing these two components will help you get the most out of your job and you'll definitely see what's in it for you.

The first part of this book is devoted to relationships at work. Relationships are of significant importance in any person's life and play a key role in nearly everything we do. Short of becoming a hermit, we can't escape relationships, so it's in our best interest to learn how to manage them successfully. This book, using examples from nature, explains the science of relationships and provides methods to help you get the most you can out of the relationships you develop.

Later in the book, we talk about what you can do to become the best you can be. That cliché has been used millions of times but becoming the best you can be is not only achievable, it's one of the hidden secrets to you finding satisfaction and success. We'll discuss ways to turn positive behavior into habits; habits you will learn to use on a continuous basis without even thinking. Doing incredible things becomes automatic when you make a habit of using positive behavior, and before long, you'll find yourself living the life you've always wanted.

I've had some successes in my life and tons of attempts that didn't turn out as originally planned. You'll notice I didn't call them failures. Failures are what happens when something mechanical breaks down. Since mechanical equipment and machinery don't have brains, they don't learn from their mistakes. Instead, once repaired, they just continue to function the same old way until the next breakdown. You and I are different. When something doesn't turn out as well as originally planned, we learn from it, we adapt, and we keep trying again until we get it right. It's that learning process and your commitment to effort that is going to make a difference for you. This book will show you how to do it.

Throughout this book I've used the term "team member". It's synonymous with "employee", but I believe "team member" takes "employee" to another level as it includes relationships as a key component. You can't have a team with only one person and companies can't exist without relationships with others. Even if a company has only one employee (the owner), relationships with clients, customers and providers move that person out of the realm of individuality. Therefore, the science of relationships is important to understand and to perfect. That's why we'll spend a lot of time talking about relationships in this book.

If you are a team member, this book will provide you with helpful advice on how to get the most out of your employment experience. Hopefully it will inspire you to become the best you can be and to move forward in your career. You may not agree with all of my theories. In fact, I hope you don't agree with everything you'll read. Instead, I hope my thoughts plant a seed from which you will sprout your own ideas and grow your own successes. All I ask is that you read this book with an open mind, take note of things you want to further contemplate and implement those portions with which you're in agreement. You are responsible for your own success. It took me years to learn that and in writing this book, I hope I have been able to share some of the lessons I've learned with you.

If you're an owner or leader in a company, I hope you take the time to read this book and understand some of the basic concepts. It will not only change your perception about what team members are thinking, but it will also help you identify the superstars, the team members you want and need on your team. Once you've read it, I encourage you to share it with everyone on your team. It's simple reading but will provide insight on how to encourage your people to become the best they can be. You may even find some of what you read helpful to you in your own job. The concepts are basic but are key to a healthy workplace.

Chapter 2: Getting the Most Out of Your Job

So, you've been at the same company for several years. You like your job and the people you work with, but you haven't really advanced. In fact, you may have seen others advancing around you while you feel stymied in the same old job. Why do you think that is? I'm sure you can come up with all kinds of reasons. Maybe your boss doesn't like you. Maybe others have been brown-nosing. Maybe you have no desire to advance or move up in the company. Can you really imagine yourself being in the exact same job 20 or 30 years from now? Probably not. Getting the most out of life is enjoying what you're doing and getting the most out of your job is going home at the end of the day feeling like you've accomplished something. It's time to start accomplishing.

I've known people who felt they accomplished something when they found ways to get out of work. In fact, they spent most of their day trying to avoid work. In reality, their work became "avoiding work". Think about that for a moment. They stressed, they strategized, they put all their effort into avoiding doing something constructive. They went home worn out and tired, just like you do, but they literally had nothing to show for their effort. If you're reading this book, I'm guessing you're not one of those people. You want something out of life. You want to feel accomplishment. You want to get ahead. If that's you, then this book is going to show you some simple ways to accomplish more, advance in your job and get ahead. The concepts aren't magical; they're really quite primitive, but few people take the time to realize them.

Relationships are a key component in helping you get ahead at work and we'll explore relationships in great detail. In fact, they are of such significant importance that your success will ultimately depend upon them. There's truth in the reality we can't do it alone. Don't be frightened. Having healthy relationships isn't that difficult. We simply need to learn how to build and use them.

So, what's in it for you? You'll probably invest a few hours reading this book. I've intentionally kept it short, not only to keep it easy to read, but more so because the concepts really aren't that complicated. It took me years to learn these simple tricks and now I get the enjoyment and sense of accomplishment of sharing them with you. As you read this book, some of the concepts may hit home and might even inspire you to try them out. Others won't sound so inspiring. That's ok. Each of us has our own style, our own characteristics and our own way of doing things. That's what sets us apart from anyone else. What's in it for you is the ability to hear about different concepts, consider them, adopt those that make sense to you and see what changes they make in your life. Hopefully they will help you along your journey and achieve the goals you've set for yourself. True satisfaction in life comes not from attaining goals that are easily reached; it comes from setting and achieving goals that can only be reached through your best efforts.

Let's get started.

Chapter 3: Symbiosis

I've always enjoyed science and nature. As I prepared to write this book, I thought about how closely relationships in nature compare to relationships in our work environments. For example, our oceans are filled with some amazing creatures. They live and thrive in waters large enough to cover two-thirds of our planet. Some of these creatures are quite small, yet they've learned the art of survival through symbiosis. From the single celled organisms to our oceans' largest whales, symbiosis plays a role.

I chose symbiosis as an important part of this book because it's a great example and directly correlates with our lives at work. Relationships are a key factor in any job, so it's a great place to start when looking how to make your job more satisfying. We'll begin by defining symbiotic relationships and providing insight as to why they are so important to everyone in a company. We'll then show you some ways to utilize symbiotic relationships to your advantage. We'll even provide tips on how to recognize unhealthy symbiotic relationships and how to address them or avoid them all together.

In order for a company to become and remain successful, relationships among people at work are critical. All members of the company must understand the importance of the symbiotic relationships that exist in the workplace. For our purposes in this book, our workforce will include team members, leaders and owners of the company. Symbiotic relationships also involve external relationships through our customers, our clients, our regulatory agents and anyone else with whom we come in contact, but in the interest of brevity, we'll stick to discussing symbiotic relationships within our workforce. The right kinds of symbiotic relationships lead to a healthy, successful company. The wrong kinds of symbiotic relationships lead to an unhealthy company, and oftentimes, a company that is on the path to a slow painful death.

To explain this phenomenon, a proper definition of symbiosis is necessary, along with an understanding of the various types of symbiotic relationships that exist. Symbiotic relationships can be both positive and negative, depending on what role you play in the relationship. The key, however, is the effect the relationship has on others.

Symbiosis is an interaction between two organisms living in close physical proximity or association. There's no better way to explain symbiotic relationships than by taking a look at our world's oceans. In the article "Symbiosis: The Art of Living Together", National Geographic does an excellent job of using nature from our oceans to describe and provide examples of the five types of symbiotic relationships:

Mutualism
Commensalism
Predation
Parasitism
Competition

Let's break each of those relationships down individually and then later tie them to our organizations at work.

Mutualism

Mutualism is a symbiotic relationship where both species or organisms benefit. A good example is the clownfish and the sea anemone. Sea anemones attach themselves to coral reefs. They trap their prey by stinging them with nematocysts, or stinging cells, which are located on their tentacles. The nematocysts release toxins when a small animal comes in contact with the anemone's tentacles. This paralyzes the stung animal which allows the anemone to easily bring it to its mouth to ingest.

While other fish succumb to these toxic stings, the clownfish secretes a mucus-like substance covering their body that prevents the nematocysts of the anemone from firing. This allows the clownfish to swim comfortably between the tentacles of the anemone without getting stung. This benefits the clownfish by allowing them to search for food near and around the anemone's tentacles. The anemone benefits because as the brightly colored clownfish swims among its tentacles, the clownfish attract other fish looking at the clownfish as a meal. These unsuspecting predators are then stung, caught and eaten by the anemone. Both the clownfish and the sea anemone benefit from this relationship.

Another example of mutualism is coral and algae. Coral provides the algae with a protected environment and the chemicals needed for algae to perform photosynthesis. The algae, in return, produce oxygen and help the coral to remove waste.

Commensalism

Commensalism is a symbiotic relationship where one species lives with, on, or in another species or host. The host neither benefits nor is harmed from the relationship. A good example of commensalism is barnacles and the humpback whale.

Barnacles attach themselves to the body of a whale and benefit when the whale carries them into plankton-rich waters, where both species feast upon the abundant microorganisms that live there. Barnacles move very slowly on their own but attaching themselves to the humpback whale allows them to travel thousands of miles. The barnacles cause no harm to the whale; they're just along for the ride.

Predation

Predation is a symbiotic relationship where the predator hunts and kills the prey. Obviously, this is healthy for the predator, but not so healthy for the prey. A good example of predation is the Orca or Killer Whale.

The Orca lives at the top of the food chain. While the Orca hunts and eats over 140 species of prey, it is not hunted by any other predator. It simply satisfies its hunger at the expense of others. Obviously, the Orca is greatly feared, and all other animals attempt to flee the area as soon as an Orca is detected. Even sharks, as ferocious and intimidating as they are, leave the waters when Orcas arrive. Attempting to make friends with an Orca is unthinkable because you never know if or when you will be considered their next meal.

Parasitism

Parasitism is a symbiotic relationship where the parasite lives with, on, or in a host species, at the expense of the host. Nematodes and leeches are parasites. They live off the host without contributing any value to the host, but often at the expense of the host. Unlike in predation, the host is not immediately killed by the parasite, but as the parasite grows and reproduces, the host may sicken and die over time.

Competition

Our last symbiotic relationship is Competition. In Competition, there is a struggle among organisms for the same limited resources. An example of competition is the relationship between corals and sponges.

Sponges are abundant in coral reefs. They anchor themselves to coral and provide habitat for shrimp, fish and other small animals. Coral relies on sunlight in order to perform photosynthesis, which provides oxygen and other nutrients to the reef. If sponges become too abundant, they block out the sunlight from the coral, thereby shutting off the needed food source of the coral. Sponges may outcompete to the point where coral can no longer survive and the reef itself becomes damaged. This is bad for both species as the sponges will also begin to die off as the coral dies until the ratio of coral and sponges on the reef begin to even out and balance is once again restored to the reef.

Ecosystem Health

Symbiotic relationships in the ocean can be useful in measuring an ecosystem's health. They can also be useful in measuring the health of a company. Just as large tracts of coral reefs have been severely damaged or destroyed due to an imbalance in symbiotic relationships, many companies have been damaged and destroyed because they failed to protect the health of the symbiotic relationships within their company.

Chapter 4: Symbiosis at Work

So how does Symbiosis apply to work? Relationships are relationships regardless of where they exist. The key to a healthy company, however, is what kind of symbiotic relationships exist within that company. We talked about how a healthy ecosystem in the ocean is dependent upon healthy symbiotic relationships. The same holds true for companies. The company must nurture heathy relationships in order to thrive. These relationships sometimes get stressed but must return to balance in order for the company to remain healthy.

Let's look at the different types of symbiotic relationships and how they affect a company.

Mutualism

Mutualism is by far the healthiest type of symbiotic relationship to have inside a company. Mutualism is based upon both organisms benefitting each other. Instead of species or organisms, we're now talking about relationships between people and different levels inside the organization. For the purpose of this book, we will look at how symbiosis affects the team member. In future books, we'll discuss how leaders and owners are affected.

In Mutualism, the Team Member, the Leader and the Owner all benefit from the relationships which exist. The Team Member benefits from feeling valued through opportunities for growth and promotion and receiving an equitable wage and benefits package in return for satisfactorily performing their duties and assignments. The Leader benefits from feeling valued, equitable wages/benefits and job growth in the organization for having led his/her team to successfully completing the tasks and assignments. The Owner benefits from having a healthy company that continues to thrive and grow, along with the personal satisfaction and compensation derived from keeping the company healthy.

In a mutualistic relationship environment, just like in our example of the clownfish and the sea anemone, everyone benefits. They work together for the benefit of each other.

Commensalism

Commensalism occurs in a corporation when a person works for a company but is only along for the ride. In other words, they're only interested in a paycheck or the benefits a company provides. They simply put in their hours. They may show up for work every day, but they only put in enough effort to get by, no more, no less. The team member working in this fashion isn't harming the company because they're still completing their assignments, but they really aren't advancing the company or contributing to the company's ability to innovate, thrive and grow. This person rides along silently on the body of the corporation, just like the barnacles rode along on the body of the whale.

The problem with a person stuck in commensalism is they will never get ahead. Its eight hours of work for eight hours of pay. Advancements and promotions are hard to come by as this type of person will never stand out and never be noticed. They simply blend in, or worse yet, hide in the shadows. They're there, but they're probably not getting any fulfillment out of their job and as such, work life to them becomes boring and a drudgery, rather than an opportunity to accomplish or a means to get ahead. They'll probably keep their job but will never be considered for opportunities or promotions.

Predation

We've all known predators at work. They don't care who they harm as long as they get what they want. While the Orca is at the top of the food chain, predators at work don't remain at the top for long. Feeding on people, stepping on them, or pushing them out of the way may seem like a good way to get ahead, but others are watching. There's a difference between being competitive and being a predator. Being competitive means, you always strive to do your best. Being a predator means, you will do anything to feed your hunger (which in this case means ego), even if it means leaving the waters around you red with the blood of others. Ironically, predators see themselves as being highly competitive. In reality, they are only highly selfish.

Initially, predators are frequently looked upon as rising stars in a company. They produce results quickly and it often appears everything they touch turns to gold. Their accomplishments can be rather impressive. For this reason, upper management may initially view this person as an up and comer. While their results are apparent, the tricks and tactics they use to achieve those results may not be so visible at first and a company may begin investing in this person as a rising star. It's only when their predatory tactics start to get revealed that the predator begins losing favor. When the company realizes they are in danger of losing other good people as a result of a predator's feeding frenzy, the charade quickly comes to a halt and the predator finds themselves no longer glimmering in the eyes of upper management.

Predators often display narcissistic tendencies and many, in fact, are true narcissists. As mentioned, due to their charm and appearance of assertively getting results, they often advance quickly, but eventually are called out when others catch onto their tactics. When Orcas come around, the rest of the creatures in the ocean swim the other way. The same holds true of predators at work. Few want to be around them fearing they could become the predator's next meal. Predators have a tendency to switch companies every few years because when their narcissistic mask of feigned charm slips and their underhanded tactics are finally exposed, they frequently move on to another company and a fresh new source of victims upon which to prey. You may find it interesting that a predator is rarely fired from a job. It may happen occasionally, but the norm is the predator will typically find another job and quit as soon as their narcissistic predatory behavior is called out. Their ego can't handle being fired, so jumping ship is often their best option.

Parasitism

A Parasite in an organization lives at the expense of the company and the people they work with. They do the least amount they can. They never volunteer and rarely get involved in projects beyond the scope of their assignment. In fact, if you're not careful, they'll get you to do their work for them. It's a one-way street with the Parasite and they can often be experts in work avoidance.

Parasites often miss a lot of days from work. They don't care to be there and are just as happy allowing someone else to complete their assignments for them during their absence. They will typically keep a very low balance in their vacation bank and will call in sick at the drop of a hat. When they are at work, they often appear busy, but no one can actually figure out what they accomplished, and the answer is usually "very little".

An inexperienced leader will often fall for the many excuses that a parasite offers for why work wasn't accomplished. They may even feel sorry for the person and move some of their workload to others, but this only results in resentment among everyone on the team. An experienced leader will detect and address parasitic tendencies quickly and prevent them from becoming a problem. Just like a parasite in nature, if not eradicated, they will eventually destroy the health of their victims and can make the entire company ill. For this reason, smart companies counsel parasites as quickly as they are detected to help them move away from this dangerous behavior. If counseling doesn't work, the parasite must be removed in order for co-workers and the company to remain healthy.

Competition

While competition can be good in a company, it must be balanced in order for the company to remain healthy. The right amount of competition makes the company better. Too much competition and the competitors begin fighting for resources.

The most effective source of competition in a company is when the team member challenges themself and encourages others to do the best they can do; to be the best they can be. This type of competition isn't threatening. On the contrary, it often inspires others to do the best they can do as well. In an inspired way, they encourage others to put forth their best effort. In sports, you often see these people pumping up other players. By pumping themselves up first, they encourage others for the benefit of the entire team.

When you're around someone who practices healthy competition by striving to be the best they can be, it can be quite contagious and before long you find yourself doing the same. In other words, healthy competition benefits everyone involved. In unhealthy competition, an unhealthy competitor will unconsciously slip into predation and feed on others.

Now that you have an understanding of how symbiotic relationships apply to work, let's examine how symbiosis affects you and your job.

Chapter 5: Basic Concepts

In the last two chapters, we looked at examples of Symbiosis in nature and how it applies to companies. Now let's look at what you, the Team Member, can do to get the most out of the symbiotic relationships at work and start working on ways to help you become the best you can be.

Have you given much thought to how much of our lives are actually spent at work? Excluding weekends, you spend about 1/3 of your time at work and 1/3 of your time sleeping. That only leaves 8 hours a day to be with your family, to play with your kids, to commute to and from work, to spend time eating, or to enjoy the things you like to do. That means you're a very busy person. We keep telling ourselves we can do with less sleep, but sooner or later that catches up with us. We can't, however, spend less than 40 hours at work if we are to maintain a full-time job. What this actually means is, weekends excluded, you are spending more time at work than you are with your family. As depressing as that may sound, there is a way to get the most out of it.

Our reasons for working vary from person to person. Some work to better themselves and get ahead. Some are there to earn enough money to keep their family afloat. Some are there for the insurance to keep their family protected. Regardless of your reason, we all need to work, so let's figure out a way to best invest our time and make it worth our while.

Remember the symbiotic relationships we described? That's what work is really all about. It's about relationships with others and how we use those relationships to our best advantage. You've probably already caught on that the best symbiotic relationship for a company is mutualism, but not everyone is wired for a mutual relationship and not everyone plays by the rules. To protect yourself, you need to understand each symbiotic style, learn how to recognize it and how to deal with it.

Before we get too far into that, we first need to discuss some basic premises that perhaps no one has ever taught you. They are fundamental, yet rarely discussed. I could go on a complete dissertation but let me simply provide you with a few basic concepts.

From the time we were born, we've been taught you can become whatever you want to be. This may or may not be entirely true. Later in this chapter, we'll talk about the difference between talent and effort. You'll quickly see that even when applying maximum effort, we may not always have the natural talent or physical characteristics to become whatever we want. There are, however, some basic concepts that have proven to be true that we can apply when it comes to getting ahead at work.

Accomplishment

Our first basic concept is at the end of the day everyone wants to feel like they accomplished something. What they sought to accomplish, however, can be either positive or negative. Let's use an example at work. Perhaps you finished a project today. Doesn't it feel good that after all your hard effort, it's finally finished? Perhaps you came up with an idea that will improve your work or the time it takes to accomplish it. Doesn't that feel awesome? Perhaps your goal today was to focus on how to get out of work and do absolutely nothing. Doesn't that feel like you wasted your day? You may have accomplished your goal of avoiding doing anything productive, but that sense of accomplishment isn't nearly as satisfying because you focused on something negative rather than something positive. Getting ahead happens when you accomplish positive things.

Let's say you decide to go camping on the weekend. You plan, you pack, you drive, you hike, you finally get there and spend the weekend camping. Doesn't it feel good that you've actually accomplished your plan? Maybe you decided your house needed to be painted. It's a lot of hard work, but doesn't it feel good once it's finished? Standing back and enjoying what you accomplished is realizing what it feels like to get ahead. It doesn't necessarily mean you got further ahead than anyone else; it means you're further ahead today than you were yesterday. You've discovered what's in it for you and you're working towards becoming the best you can be.

Life Is to Be Enjoyed

The question remains, "Why do you want to get ahead; to become the best you can be?" The answer to that is quite simple. Life is to be enjoyed and you can't enjoy life if you feel like you're walking in wet cement. If you continue to trudge through life, your mind and your body won't hold up. Eventually you will tire and completely give up. If you see yourself walking in wet cement, now is the time to do something about it. Now is the time to refocus your goals and start enjoying life. Imagine what it would be like to enjoy what you do, to make significant accomplishments, to look forward to advancement, to get ahead. It's within your control.

You've heard the term "in a slump". It usually applies to pro athletes. They've suddenly found themselves in a position where very little is going right and what's going wrong has put them in a downhill spiral. You may have found yourself in the same position at one point in your life. How did you get out of it? It wasn't by hiding in your room and doing nothing. It was by putting forth more effort to break the pattern around you. When a pro golfer gets in a slump, the first thing their coaches tell them is to hit the driving range. Is that to improve their swing? No. At this point in their career, their swing has already been established. They hit the driving range to remind themselves they have the talent and ability to get through it. Putting forth a little extra effort reminds them that they have what it takes to get through this slump; they just have to convince their mind it is worth it. That's probably how you got through your slump as well. A pro golfer in a slump doesn't put their clubs away for six months and then one day wake up feeling better and decide to hit the tour again. They work through their slump by applying maximum effort.

To enjoy life, you have to feel the satisfaction of accomplishment. It doesn't mean you have to discover the cure for cancer, although that would be amazing. It means accomplishing something you wanted to accomplish. You went camping. You painted the house. You completed a project at work. Accomplishment is the seed that will inspire you to do even more.

Chapter 6: Secrets of Getting Ahead

Since this book focuses on work, how to get ahead and how relationships help us to succeed, we'll discuss the secrets of getting ahead as they pertain to work, but you'll find these same techniques will also apply to other aspects of your life, as well.

If you take these secrets to heart, attempt to apply them on a regular basis and actually work to make them habits, I can assure you that you will accomplish more, you'll got more satisfaction from your job and opportunities will open up for you.

The secrets are:

- Utilize your God-Given talents to their fullest potential
- Utilize maximum effort to subsidize any areas where your talents aren't sufficient
- Get past the limitations your mind tries to set for you
- Work for the right company, the company that sees and appreciates your efforts
- Take control of your career path
- Speak from your heart
- Remember that perceptions can be inaccurate, so always attempt to view them from different angles
- Utilize your principles as a chain of reasoning
- Rely on your values and always return to them in times of doubt
- Work Through Issues
- Integrity – the only thing a person will ever truly own

- Respect

Over the next few chapters, we'll break each of these secrets down and discuss how you can use them to gain more satisfaction in your job and perhaps increase your chances for opportunities.

Chapter 7: God-Given Talents

When my daughters were young, self-esteem was the concept deemed of utmost importance in dealing with young people. The theory came from an idea that children's self-esteem should be protected, and they should never have to compare themselves with others. While this line of thinking may have helped improve self-esteem, it suppressed those with talent and bred mediocrity. The child on the soccer field who possessed more talent or gave more effort than others received the same recognition as those kids who simply showed up. Players quickly learned their talents and best efforts were not recognized, or at least weren't appreciated. Soon a mediocre effort was the most that could be expected from any of the players. Take away recognition or any incentive to excel and mediocrity is all you'll have left.

Did God really give us talents to have them suppressed or wasted? I don't think so. He gave us talents to utilize, to make our lives more enjoyable and abundant. So why do we find our talents so frequently oppressed?

The idea of talent is to this day a controversial subject because the politically correct view is to value all people the same regardless of talent or ability. But let's face it, some people were born with more talent and more ability than others. At 5'9", I'm never going to be an NBA basketball player. I not only don't have the talent, but I also don't have the physical attributes to play at that level. I accept that and it doesn't hurt my self-esteem to do so. In fact, it helps my self-esteem because it makes me focus on the talents I actually possess. I can become good at being me. I will never be good at being you.

So back to the highly talented soccer player who gave his/her best effort. Imagine how he/she felt coming off the field knowing they had used their talents and had done their best only to see their efforts ignored. Do you really think they are going to continue putting out at that level of effort? Chances are they won't. Instead of furthering that soccer player's talents, we have encouraged them to give less, to be more like everyone else. We have suppressed them.

What happens when you remove the high and low data points on a graph? You get a centralized field of data, not necessarily accurate, but statistically common. Instead of striving to hit high points, you focus on maintaining the data between the preconceived lines. Why do more than the preconceived lines ask you to do? After all, any successes or areas in which you excel will only be tossed out in order to preserve the statistical data. When you throttle back talent, so no one feels offended, you are left with a centralized field of data. You breed mediocrity. No more shining stars, no more up and comers and no more innovative ideas that allow a team or a company to stay ahead of their competition. You get a nice-looking graph but take away any incentive for anyone to perform higher than the current expectations.

There's a decades long controversy going on in our schools. It involves the rate at which different children learn. If you have a class of 30 kids, statistically 10-20 percent of those students will be fast learners and 10-20 percent of those students will be slow learners. That leaves 60-80 percent of the students as average learners. In other words, not all students learn at the same rate. If the class is geared toward average learners, the fast learners will become bored and the slow learners will fall behind.

One solution for this was to develop gifted-learning classes for the fast learners so they could continue to develop and to utilize remedial classes for those that needed additional time and help. This seemed like a great idea, but what do you think happened? Parents complained because their average learner wasn't considered for the gifted-learning program and parents of slower learners complained because their child was placed in the remedial class to give them more help. As a result, many school districts abandoned these programs.

Now I know there often were problems with who was selected for these classes. Bias, favoritism and nepotism all reared their ugly heads and gave these programs a bad name, but in my view, breeding mediocrity is not what I want for my child. And if my child needed additional help, then give them all the help they need. By the way, the bias, favoritism and nepotism didn't come from the kids; it came from adults not acting like adults.

Address the structural issues and make these programs work for the benefit of the kids. Give the fast-learners opportunities to grow their talents. Give the slower learners any specialized help they need. We should always strive to help everyone reach their fullest potential.

So, what does all of this have to do with you? God has provided you with your own set of unique talents. In fact, we all have talents in certain areas, but none of us have talents in all areas. I can hone my talents if I was born with them, but I can't create a talent if I wasn't born with that talent to begin with. One of the first secrets of getting ahead is to make sure we utilize the talents God has given us. That doesn't necessarily mean that every talent is applicable at all times, but if it is applicable, then we should use it. If you have a beautiful singing voice, I'm not quite sure how that will help you as a paralegal, but why not put that talent to good use in your spare time by singing in a choir or performing with a local band. If you've never experienced a room full of people applauding after you've finished singing a song, you don't know what you're missing.

If you have a God-given talent, find a way to use it and enjoy the abundance of satisfaction it brings. If God gave you the talent of being a leader, then utilize those talents and set your career goals accordingly. To become the best we can be, we have to utilize the talents God has given us and the more we use those talents, the more satisfying life becomes.

What if I don't have a lot of talent in a certain area, but need to utilize those skills in my job? Just as I will never be an NBA basketball star, we can't create talent if we weren't born with it. We simply can't pick and choose our God-given talents and we can't control when we are lacking a particular talent. What we can control, however, is effort.

Chapter 8: Maximum Effort

Before I move on to effort, let me give you one more example of talent. Michael Jordan was one of the greatest basketball players that ever lived. When he finished his first basketball career, he went on to play Major League Baseball. He subsequently went back to basketball and continued his illustrious career. He's also pretty good at golf and pretty much anything else he does. There is no doubt in my mind that if Michael Jordan and I were to sit down to a game of checkers, he would whip me in that as well. Why? Because he has the mindset of healthy competition and maximum effort. Now if I look hard enough, I bet I have a talent that Michael Jordan doesn't possess, but even a competition with him on my talent would be difficult because Michael learned how to give maximum effort. Whatever he does, he's going to do at the best of his ability. I don't know if Michael has any musical skills, but you can bet if he were encouraged to sing, he would sing with his whole heart and soul, regardless of his level of talent. Maximum effort.

All of this is leading up to how do YOU get the most out of work. You'll notice "YOU" was emphasized. It was done so for a reason. You have many talents. Hopefully some of those talents are usable every day for you at work. If so, you're already a step ahead. What do you do, however, if you have average talent? It doesn't matter if you have a lot of talent, average talent, or little talent, the answer is the same. You control effort. Earlier I mentioned you can't create talent; you can only hone it. Of course, you should take advantage of your talents and use them whenever possible, but it's your level of effort that is completely up to you.

How do you think Michael Jordan learned maximum effort? He probably had a few coaches, but he did it mainly by pushing himself to become the best he can be and never settling with a mediocre effort. He learned that effort can overcome talent challenges. He learned: to get better, you have to want to become the best you can be.

Maybe you're in a job that isn't your dream job. Maybe you're just pulling down a paycheck. Maybe you don't think you have the talent to advance. I want to show you a way to get to your dream job, a way to start a career instead of just pulling down a paycheck, a way to take advantage of the talents you have and to use effort to overcome the talents you might be lacking. Best of all, it's all done through effort and your understanding and use of symbiotic relationships.

What would happen if you went into work today and decided to give the best possible effort you could? What would happen if you volunteered for special projects instead of being assigned them? What would happen if you suddenly started helping someone else that was struggling? What would happen if, using a phrase stolen from one of my old co-workers, you suddenly became one of the "Cool Kids"? Your life would probably change, wouldn't it? Let's start changing it.

Effort is a mindset, but it's also habit. The more you begin to maximize effort; the easier effort will become until one day it comes naturally. Do you think Michael Jordan does anything today without putting forth his maximum effort? I doubt it. He probably brushes his teeth with maximum effort. He acquired that ability; has made it a habit and it has helped him through his entire career.

To train yourself to maximum effort, start with your next task. Instead of just completing it, think about how you can do it better. How can you do it more accurately? How can you improve it? How can you make it easier? Then do it! When you're finished, sit back and look at your achievement. Didn't it feel good to do the best you possibly could? Now try it on your next task. Each task you do today, give it your maximum effort, then do it all over again tomorrow. Just like an athlete trains their body and mind, you'll be training yourself to become the best you can be. Soon you will be giving maximum effort to everything you do. Make maximum effort a habit in your life and you'll be amazed at what you can accomplish and the opportunities it will open up for you.

Here's one more trick. Do the task you dread the most first. I know there's a tendency to procrastinate and push those least-liked tasks to the end of the day, but did you realize how much stress you're actually causing yourself by procrastinating? Have you ever found yourself faced with a task that you dread, but must do? I bet you continued to worry and fret about it until you finally tackled it. Early on in my career, I did the same thing. I would push these tasks to the end of the day and fretted about them all day long. I would actually ruin my entire day, because while I was doing other things, my mind kept slipping back to the task I dreaded the most. What I learned is 9 times out of 10, the task wasn't nearly as bad as I thought it was going to be, so I spent my day worrying about nothing. Maybe it was a phone call, maybe it was delivering bad news, or maybe it was a task I dreaded but had to complete. In any event, if I performed that task first thing in the morning, it was off my plate and I could quit worrying about it. There were times when the task wasn't pleasant, but there was relief knowing I had it off my plate and could now get on with my day. Do the dreaded tasks first and you'll be amazed how much easier the rest of your day goes.

So, what does this have to do with symbiotic relationships? In mutualism, both species benefit from the relationship. If you're giving forth maximum effort, you're helping yourself become the best you can be. At the same time, you're helping your co-workers, your leader and the owner of the company. It's a Win-Win-Win-Win. When you consistently give your best effort, it will be noticed and when it comes time for promotion, guess who they will be considering? They look for the top producers and the people that give maximum effort. By giving maximum effort and constantly striving to be the best you can be, you're not only helping your company; you're also helping yourself. Suddenly the "what's in it for you" becomes apparent.

There's one other thing I noticed about giving maximum effort. Have you ever glanced at the clock while working and felt like time was standing still? I found when I gave maximum effort, the opposite happened. Not only did the day fly by, but I often wished there were a few more hours in the day because I wasn't quite yet finished with something I was working on. I became absorbed by my project and doing the best I could do on it, time was no longer something I dreaded, but something I actually cherished. I'd go home at the end of the day feeling like I actually accomplished something and there's no better feeling than that.

Here's one more bit of help. When you start to focus on maximum effort, be careful not to slip into thinking it's all about you. You can't survive without relationships and relationships at work are vitally important. As you pursue maximum effort, don't allow yourself to slip into predation, parasitism, or unhealthy competition. To become the best you can be means being able to effectively work with others. Give maximum effort to working on mutualism and healthy competition where your efforts help others, and their efforts help yours. Being a team player who works towards the benefit of everyone will win you the friendship, respect and support of those around you.

If you see someone with a special talent or is putting forth maximum effort, learn from them. Compliment them on their effort and ability. Don't be afraid to ask questions. Surround yourself with maximum effort people and you'll find yourself giving maximum effort yourself. A.D. Posey, a well-known author of poems and quotations once said, "Surround yourself with those conducive to you being your highest self." I truly believe this. If you want to become the best you can be, you have to surround yourself with people of like mind and are willing to give and receive help.

Chapter 9: Limitations of the Mind

Can you really train yourself to become the best you can be? The mind is an amazing organ and is capable of doing things we don't yet understand. At the same time, the mind can be quite limiting. It can fool us into thinking we have limitations or close our mind to trying new things.

I have a good friend who is a marathon runner. She always enjoyed running, but always felt a marathon was out of her reach. After a few miles, she would feel the aches and pains, she would feel herself getting out of breath, so she would stop. She told herself she just didn't have the ability to run a marathon. In the back of her mind, however, a small flame continued to burn. She wanted to prove to herself she could do it. The next time she went out running, she ran a little further than normal. She found herself getting out of breath and her mind was telling her to stop, but she didn't. She pushed through it. She gradually ran further and further and today is now running several marathons a year. Her body was capable of running much further than her mind was telling her she could. It was limiting her. Once she proved those false limitations were wrong, she was running marathons. She was becoming the best she could be.

Here's another example. I've never been much of a drinker. I might have a beer every once in a while, but just really never had the desire to drink. My doctor told me it might be a good idea for me to have a glass of wine every once in a while. At that time, the going theory was that wine was rich in antioxidants and good for your heart. We later learned that theory came more from the wine industry than the medical field, but it worked as many more people had an excuse to drink wine. In any event, I knew nothing about wine, but decided I needed to learn.

I turned to friend of mine who was a wine aficionado. He knew a lot about wine, and I asked him to teach me. When I asked, he said he would be glad to teach me, but it was June and he suggested waiting until November. He explained a person will feel warmth as they swallow a sip of wine and they will find it much more satisfying to learn to drink wine when the outside temperature is cooler.

That November, my wine lessons began. Since I wanted to drink red wines for their antioxidant advantage, he suggested starting with a good dry Cabernet Sauvignon. There was a reason for his selection. The first-time people drink wine, their mind often fools them. Prior to taking a sip, your mind is already telling you that since wine is made from grapes, which is a fruit, it should be sweet to the taste. As a result, your first sip of a dry wine is rather surprising and sometimes less than enjoyable. Instead of something sweet, you get something that may be a bit bitter. In order to get around this, prior to sipping the wine, you have to convince your mind to not expect sweetness, but rather to search the wine for what flavors you're able to discern in it.

Many people think wine is made only from grapes. Grapes are indeed a major component, but wines are flavored with many different kinds of fruits like plums, cherries, blackberries and a host of others. It can also be flavored with such flavors as chocolate, tobacco and spices. It may carry tannins from the barrel in which it matured. Once you convince your mind to forget sweet and instead, search for flavors, you can really start enjoying wine.

What if I had started with a sweet red wine? My mind would have tasted the sweetness and associated sweet with wine. It undoubtedly would have prevented me from tasting or experiencing anything else. A sip of a nice dry Cabernet Sauvignon would have been awful, and I would have avoided it like the plague. I would never have learned to enjoy the varied tastes and flavors of really good wines. Instead, I followed through with my friend's suggestion and started with a good dry red wine. I pushed through the limitations of my mind and now enjoy various kinds of wines for their unique and distinctive flavors.

Although it's sometime easier said than done, you can overcome the false limitations your mind often tries to instill in you. It just takes effort, repetition and perseverance. The first few times I took a sip of wine, I needed to remind myself it wouldn't be sweet, and I needed to search for flavors. Now it comes automatically. The first few times my friend went out running after discovering her mind was limiting her, she felt herself breathing laboriously and even wanted to stop, but now she knows not to honor those false limitations.

Don't let your mind limit you from becoming the best you can be or enjoying life to its fullest. Push those limits and see what you're really capable of doing

Chapter 10: Work for the Right Company

Remember that dream job you've always wanted? Maybe it's at the company at which you're currently working. If that's the case, your maximum effort philosophy will certainly get you noticed. In fact, you might just find out that dream job you always wanted was right in front of you and within reach, only you were previously unable to see it, or you were allowing your mind to set false limitations. Now that you're focused, a lot of things will become easier and your path much clearer.

Once you've eliminated false limitations in your mind and have become a maximum effort team member, it's time to look at the benefits of your symbiotic relationship with your current employer. Hopefully you're already working for a boss and a company that truly appreciates your efforts and abilities. If that's the case, you're on the fast track to growth, development and promotion. Good bosses and good companies recognize talent and provide those who put forth maximum effort with opportunities and challenges that will further their careers. Just keep doing your best and remain prepared for the opportunities to open. You're at the right company.

What if your dream job isn't available at your current company? As you grow your career with your current company, you'll not only become more valuable to them, but to other companies as well, for you will have learned new skills and gained invaluable experience in the process. In addition, because you've been practicing maximum effort, it's now become a habit, which will make you much more attractive to any company. You'd be amazed at how many times a dream job pops up because someone you once worked with, who is now at another company, remembered the amazing effort you put forth while working with you. They now want you on their team at their new company. It's all about relationships. That's why establishing mutualistic and healthy competitive relationships is so important. Your maximum effort will get you noticed; your relationships will open doors.

Whatever you do, don't fall into the trap of withholding effort or harming relationships because you don't feel you're being treated properly where you currently work. I've seen many people ruin their career because they quit putting forth effort in retribution for their opinion that their company didn't appreciate them. That only harms you. Not only will the people you work with see you withholding effort, but so will your company and the brakes will be applied on any plans they may have had for your development. Remember that maximum effort can become a habit and it will come without even thinking about it if you allow it to do so. Intentionally withholding effort out of spite will destroy all the work you've already done to make your maximum effort a habit. Your maximum effort and healthy relationships are the keys to your success, whether at your current job or any you may wish to pursue. Damaging relationships or reducing effort is an expensive price to pay to your career. If you think you're getting back at your employer by doing so, think again. You are only damaging yourself and your ability to advance your career in the future.

What if you're at a good company, but your boss doesn't seem to recognize your talents? If that's the case, then first look inward. Are you truly giving every assignment the best effort you possibly could? Looking inside yourself isn't easy and you won't always appreciate everything you see, but it's a vital step to helping you become the best you can be. Why start there? We have the ability to correct our own deficiencies; correcting the deficiencies of others is much, much harder, if even possible. Looking inward first assures that you are not the problem. Our minds are quick to point fingers at others, but oftentimes what has happened is a result of something we did or failed to do. We can control ourselves; we can't control others, so doesn't it just make sense to start with the easiest task first?

It's often been said that we are our own worst critics and I believe that to be true. Don't be hard on yourself; be honest with yourself. If after looking inside, you honestly feel that you are giving it your best effort, then it's time for The Talk with your boss.

There may be a host of reasons why you are currently working at a specific company. Maybe it's because they have a reputation for treating their people well. Maybe it's because it was the only company hiring for your specific skills. Maybe it's proximity; it's close to where you wish to live. Whatever the reason, consider those things in your assessment of "Is this the right company for me?", but don't make them the only parameters you consider. In other words, don't jump ship because the grass looks greener somewhere else. In most cases, it's only greener for a season. That's why so many people return to companies they had previously left.

On the other hand, don't continue to stay at a company if your efforts aren't appreciated and rewarded. If you're giving maximum effort and truly practice mutualism and healthy competition, but don't feel appreciated or don't see a future for you, then it's time to look to see what else might be available. Do your research. Talk to team members of any company you might be considering. Learn what makes the company tick, what are their philosophies and tenets, and how they treat their people. If you see opportunities at another company that aren't available to you at your current job, then go for it. Your days of just pulling down a paycheck are over. Now that you are focused on relationships and becoming the best you can be, it's time to find a company that fits your needs.

Chapter 11: Take Control of Your Career Path

A large majority of the workforce stumbled upon their current career. Although there are some who followed their dreams and ended up doing exactly what they originally planned to do, many of us simply found ourselves headed down a career path that may or may not have anything to do with our original dreams or education.

Coming out of high school, I wanted to be a physician. After two years in college, I had an opportunity to attend paramedic school and become one of my state's first paramedics. Thinking this would be a good path for me to show my dedication to the medical profession, I put a temporary halt to pre-med and completed paramedic school. When I finished, I quickly found out that I wasn't able to serve as a paramedic on the squads of my hometown due to union rules involving our local fire department. Instead, I obtained a job as an industrial paramedic at a local manufacturing plant.

While serving as an industrial paramedic, I became interested in management, went back to college, finished my degree and I found myself deeply imbedded in a career path of industrial management. It was a great career for me, but far different from the medical profession I had originally planned. Talking with people over the years, I found a majority of people followed a similar path. Their original intentions were somehow put aside, and they one day found themselves in another career altogether. Some may call it chance. I call it God knowing what is best for us and providing the opportunities for us to get there.

You may have found yourself in a similar situation. Did you have any idea you would be doing what you're doing 10 years ago? Probably not. But regardless of what profession you're in or career path you've taken, you never want to leave your career in the hands of someone else. You own it and you have to plot that path. Once you decide the path you want to take, it's up to you to continue driving it forward. That means being assertive and having honest and sincere conversations with your boss.

So, what's the best way to have a career discussion with your boss? It starts with you being assertive enough to ask for it. Remember to remain flexible. Just because you requested to speak with your boss doesn't mean he/she is able to drop everything and give you the time you want immediately. On the other hand, don't let them off the hook by just agreeing to someday sit down with you. Push for a date and time that will work for both of you. This is important to you, and it should be, but be reasonable if your boss isn't immediately available. Use the time instead to jot down your thoughts and gather your ideas.

Your goal in this meeting is to have a frank and honest conversation with your boss regarding your career. Sincerity, honesty and tact are the keys. Chances are your boss already has a plan laid out for you and you need to hear what that plan entails, but you not only have input into your career plan; you have ownership. That means listening to what plans your boss spells out, but not being afraid to express your views and sharing the plan you feel is right for you. You have a stake in the outcome of this meeting; therefore, make sure you get to the things that are important to you. Talk about your goals and how you'd like your career path to go over the next several years. Then ask your boss for their thoughts regarding your plans.

Talk about your strengths and how you can put them to better use. Ask your boss if they agree with the strengths you have identified and discuss any differences. Talk about your weaknesses and ask your boss for help in addressing them. Your boss can't read your mind and you can't read theirs, so make sure you get everything on the table and encourage your boss to do the same. Use your notes to make sure all your points are adequately covered. Remember, your plan may not exactly coincide with the plan your boss has for you, so talk about how you can bring those plans closer together. The point of this talk is not to necessarily come to an agreement on every point, but rather to get the points on the table and agree to work on them together. If you're successful in doing this, you'll have gone a long way in solidifying your career and your relationship with your boss.

Over the course of my career and in a management role, I've often been amazed at how frequently I have assumed a career path for someone only to find out I was completely wrong in the path I thought they wanted. I learned, instead of assuming, to ask each person what they wanted to do and what talents they wanted to grow. I must admit, I've been wrong more than I've been right in assuming a career path for someone. The only way to know for sure is to ask them what they truly want to do.

Jean was an up and comer. She had great people skills and was assertive enough to go after any challenge. She was the Administrative Office Manager, but I saw great things in her future. I saw a career path for her that would take her into other levels and eventually to a general manager of a facility. I spoke with her about these opportunities, but I failed to ask her what she really wanted. Unbeknownst to me, she didn't want to disappoint me, so she didn't share her feelings during our discussion. She simply went along with my plan for her. I had decided to start her growth by challenging her to learn more of the duties of our plant manager. I saw the plant manager position as a logical step in her path toward a general manager. I wanted her to work closely with our plant manager and begin picking up the knowledge she would need to be promoted into that position, should it ever open up.

Several weeks into this plan, I saw something strange happening. I normally held one-on-one meetings every week with Jean, but she began cancelling our meetings due to conflicts. I didn't think anything of it at first because I knew she was busy, but by the time she cancelled the third meeting in a row, I recognized we may have a problem. During my next one-on-one with the plant manager, I asked him how Jean was progressing. To my surprise, he informed me she wasn't giving it much effort. My eyes really opened up wide when I heard this. Jean, my rising star, was not putting forth an effort? This is a person who always gave 110%. I realized I had a problem. Instead of scheduling a meeting with Jean, I dropped into her office and asked if she had a few minutes to talk. I could tell she was a little uncomfortable, but she honored my request. I asked her how things were going, and she said, "fine". I asked her how she was enjoying picking up new plant manager skills. There was dead silence. I broke the silence by saying, "Are things not going well? Is there something wrong?" I told her I had talked to the plant manager and it was his perception that she wasn't really into learning plant manager skills. At that point, Jean began to open up. She told me she really had no interest in becoming a plant manager; her heart was in the administrative office. She said she went along with my plan because she didn't want to disappoint me. She said as she began to spend time with the plant manager, she quickly realized how much she loved administration and how little she wanted to go into plant management, but she was afraid to tell me.

I have to tell you this was a wake-up call for me and I had to do a lot of soul-searching. Not only did I assume a career path for someone without really knowing what they wanted, but I also somehow left the impression that I would be disappointed in her if she chose not to follow the path I had laid out for her. It was quite a learning experience for me and one I greatly needed.

A leader should never assume a career path for a team member; they should discuss a career path with that team member. More importantly, a good leader creates an environment where team members are comfortable discussing any issues or concerns. Jean was worried about disappointing me. I disappointed myself by not having listened, but instead assumed. Once I knew what her true interests were, we were able to assemble a career path that properly suited her needs.

Remember this as you talk to your boss. He/she may already have an idea in their head about the path your career should take. If so, listen to it, keep an open mind, but express your ideas and feelings as well. Don't be afraid to share your true thoughts and feelings and never follow a career path against your will simply because someone else wants you to do so. Work together with your boss to develop a career path that meets both of your needs. You'll both be better off.

Now what happens if it doesn't go so well? What if your boss has an entirely different plan than yours and isn't a direction you care to take? Don't get upset, get pragmatic. It's time to deal with this in a realistic and sensible way. If you can't mesh the paths both you and your boss have laid out into an acceptable plan for both of you, then you need to take some time to digest all that you have discussed. Don't make any sudden decisions. Don't back yourself into a corner by inferring threats like suggesting you may have to look elsewhere for a job. Simply understand that your visions don't coincide and give yourself time to think through your options.

Whatever you do, don't get into a heated discussion. You can't control others; you can only control how you react or respond to others. We've all been in a situation where a discussion doesn't go the way we intended. At that point, we've already begun losing control. Control of a discussion doesn't belong to the person who yells the loudest; it belongs to the person that is able to keep the other person at the table. That's your goal because you can't come to a mutual agreement if you're not both sitting at the table. Sitting at the table may mean ending the current discussion, thinking through what was said, evaluating your options and getting back together to finish the discussion at another time. That doesn't mean you have to give in to their demands. It means you have to be strong, tactful and savvy enough to keep the discussion going, albeit at another time and after you've had the opportunity to gather your thoughts.

The way to do that is to speak from your heart. Tell your boss you hadn't really thought about the plan they had laid out for you and you need some time to think it through. Let them know that although you'd really like to follow your own plan, you'd like some time to consider everything that was discussed. If you're truly speaking from your heart, chances are your boss will give you the time you need to think everything through.

Ultimately, if your boss isn't concerned about your desires and continues to push you into a career path that you have no interest in pursuing, then it's time to find the right boss or the right company that is interested in advancing the career you want.

Chapter 12: Speak from Your Heart

Have you ever had a conversation with someone where you realized they were speaking from their heart? When you know they genuinely believe what they are saying and are truly sincere, it's pretty hard to question their sincerity or refute what they are telling you. When you speak from your heart with your boss or anyone else, you convey the message so much better. When your boss sees how much you believe in what you are saying, chances are they will give much more credence to your conversation. Your boss may not always agree on what you are saying, but if the words come from your heart, they will carry much more weight than if they are coming from your mind.

Just like maximum effort can become a habit, speaking from the heart can also become a habit and it can change your life in some very powerful ways.

From the time we learn to speak, we are coached in what to say. Your mother said, "Say Mama" and you learned to say, "Mama." From there you went on to school. You learned lessons and recited what you learned. You learned that if you said the right words, it made others happy and if you said the wrong words, it made others sad or even mad. You became conditioned. You were conditioned to say what you thought you ought to say rather than saying what is truly in your heart.

Speaking from the heart isn't easy. It makes us vulnerable. It makes us tap and ultimately reveal our emotions. That's not always comfortable. When we speak from the heart, we speak what is true to us and that is where the real value comes in. We speak our truth. Granted, what we believe isn't always what others believe and there's the possibility that our belief could be wrong, but if we have the courage to speak from the heart and reveal our truths, we give others the opportunity to hear our views and see a glimpse of how important those views really are to us.

Imagine a world for a minute where you always spoke from your heart. Whenever you spoke, you had conviction and you truly believed everything you said. Not only that, but everyone else understood every word you said was sincere, honest, genuine and what you believed. How different our world would be. For once, conditioning wouldn't come into play. We wouldn't say what we thought people wanted to hear, but rather what we really wanted to say. We wouldn't be saying things just to say them, but rather because we believed them.

Not long ago, I cooked my wife and I a meal. I spent a lot of time preparing it, but I'll be the first to tell you that I wasn't overly pleased with the outcome. It didn't have as much flavor as I would have liked. After my wife took a couple of bites, she said "This is good." At first, I thought she was crazy but then I realized she was just trying to be supportive and polite. What I needed was tactful honesty. Of course, I would have been devastated if she had said "This has no taste", but it would probably have been an honest comment. I would have preferred if she would have said something like "I know you spent a lot of time on this and I appreciate that. It isn't bad, but it could use more flavor." Now those are tactfully honest words I could do something with.

When she said, "This is good", I realized she was trying not to hurt my feelings, but it suddenly made me wonder how many other times in the past she had said kind words that really weren't honest but were said only to avoid hurting my feelings. When we bought our house, was she really not happy with it but agreed only to avoid hurting my feelings? When I decided to accept a job, did she agree only to avoid hurting my feelings? When I asked her to marry me, did she agree only to avoid hurting my feelings? See where I'm going with this?

The worst part was it made me realize how many times I had done the same thing to her. When she asks me about what she's wearing, I always respond with a positive supporting response, regardless of what I truly think. I've been using conditioning instead of speaking from my heart. I remember one time she asked me how she looked before going out and I told her she looked nice. Sometime during her outing, she walked past a mirror and wasn't pleased with how she looked. When she got home, she said "Why didn't you tell me?" Now if truth be told, I would probably never tell her that outfit didn't look the best on her. However, I could have come up with a tactful, yet honest and sincere way of telling her she might look better in something else. After all, she asked for my opinion, not my conditioned response that provided no helpful information. I should have just spoken from my heart in a way that she knew I was trying to help, not criticize. I pride myself in speaking from the heart when something is important to me, but I often fail when conditioning gets in the way. That's something I will continue to work on. In the mutualistic relationship I have with my wife, it's beneficial to both of us if I am honest and speak from the heart, even when I've been conditioned to respond in another way.

What is it about speaking from the heart that is so important? It establishes a pattern in a way you communicate with others that assures them what you say is what you actually believe. Coupled with tact, they can depend on you to always be honest and genuine with them. It's key to any relationship and more so in a mutualistic relationship when you're relying so heavily on each other.

The key, however, is tact. Speaking from the heart doesn't give you the right to just say whatever's on your mind. Just because you believe something doesn't mean it's absolutely true. Instead of a belief, it may simply be a perception. Tact is a way to discuss your beliefs while remaining open to different beliefs of others and the possibility of viewing situations from different angles. It means watching out for someone's feelings while still conveying your thoughts.

Tact isn't always easy, and some people are better at it than others, but it's something that is necessary in any mutualistic relationship. Tact includes listening to the points of views of others and not judging, but rather seeking to understand so you can make better decisions together. It means discussing thoughts, beliefs and ideas in a non-threatening way and being open enough to adjust your thoughts when seeing something from a different angle. It reveals different points of view and puts them on the table for discussion. It means understanding the difference between a belief and a perception. It means speaking from the heart and sharing views in a way that is mutually beneficial to both of you.

Chapter 13: The Inaccuracy of Perception

For years I've shared with coworkers my concept on perception. Understanding about perceptions has helped me prevent a lot of issues. Perception is truly in the mind of the beholder. To them, their perception is accurate, and they use that perception to interpret, analyze and act. If you believe someone's perception is incorrect, nothing you say will change their mind. The only thing that will change someone's perception is if they see it from another point of view and determine that their original perception may have been inaccurate.

Here's how a perception develops. I witnessed something one or more times and, in my mind, I formed an opinion about what I saw. Now every time I see that same thing or something similar, I'm going to apply my theory based upon my original perception.

As an example, let's say you met someone for the first time. Let's call him Tom. During that meeting, Tom came off as standoffish, perhaps even arrogant or rude. You formed a perception or opinion about him based upon your observation. No matter how many times someone else tries to convince you that Tom isn't arrogant or rude, you're not going to believe them because you saw it for yourself and your perception was formed. The only way you'll ever change that perception is if you see it for yourself that your original perception was incorrect.

You formed your original perception based upon one point of view or one angle. If you happen to run into Tom at another time and this time Tom is very warm and kind, you may alter your perception slightly or you may keep your original perception in the back of your mind until you see him on multiple occasions differently from your first encounter. Perhaps the first time you met Tom, he was having a bad day, or something occurred just prior to you meeting him that caused him to come off as arrogant or rude. Perhaps that was uncommon for Tom, but you just happened to catch him at a bad time, and you formed a perception based upon that one encounter. Again, nothing anyone could say was going to change your mind; you had to see it for yourself that Tom was different from how you originally perceived him to be.

Have you ever argued with a teenage over something and nothing you say will change their mind? That's because they have a perception. Oftentimes we think teenagers argue just for the sake of arguing, but in reality, it's because they have observed something from one point of view, and they are convinced that's the way it is and always will be.

For example, if a teenager picks up from television or social media that smoking makes you look cool, they may form a perception that smoking is cool and chances are, will try it for themselves. Nothing you say is going to change that teenager's mind. They saw it from one point of view and that's exactly what they are going to believe. No matter how many times you try to discuss it, you will never change their mind.

To change their perception, you have to get them to look at it from a different angle. Leaving pamphlets or books around isn't going to cut it as people have a tendency to only read things that support their opinions. Perhaps you know someone who has battled or is battling lung cancer caused by years of smoking. Introduce your teenager to this person and allow them to tell your teen how much they wish they had never started smoking in the first place. If you don't know of anyone, search YouTube or the internet. There are plenty of testimonies online from people that are willing to share their stories to help prevent others from going through their tragedy. Watch these videos together so your teenager knows you are investing in them. Now you've provided a completely different point of view for your them. If it sinks in deeply enough, chances are your teen will change their perception on smoking. Remember, words won't change a perception, viewing something from a different angle might.

Chapter 14: Utilize Your Principles

Throughout our lives, we use perceptions, principles and values to guide our actions. What's the difference between a perception, a principle and a value?

As previously stated, a perception is a belief you develop based upon one or more observations. Perceptions can be accurate, but they can also be extremely inaccurate, as well. If I perceive someone as being a bad person and that causes me to stay away from them, that may be a good thing. However, if my perception is inaccurate and that person is really a good person, I may be missing out on an opportunity to get to know them, to learn from them, to share with them, and perhaps even enjoy an amazing friendship with them.

A principle, on the other hand, is a fundamental belief that serves as a chain of reasoning and has proven accurate to you over and over again. Principles help guide you through life. You will use your principles to make life changing decisions and they will help keep you on a firm path for as long as that principle remains important. Principles, however, may change at any time in the course of your life and you will continue to develop new principles throughout your life.

Let's use the example of a young boy. We'll call him Jack. At the age of 8 or 9, Jack is learning all sorts of things. In some boys, at that age, sports start becoming more and more important and Jack is no exception. His dad was a high school and college standout football player and Jack sees football in his future. He learns all the skills, he practices hard, he follows his favorite NFL team. Football is his life. One of the principles he develops is he will work hard to become an NFL player. He'll live football until he reaches his dream. Football is now a principle that is guiding his life. Because of his hard work, Jack indeed becomes a Peewee football star. He plays high school football and again is one of the stars of the team. But then something changes. In his senior year in high school, Jack realizes what he really wants to become is a medical doctor. During his football career, he suffered a minor injury to his knee and an orthopedic physician helped him get through it. Jack became so impressed with the work this doctor was doing that Jack decided to pursue a career in the medical field.

He continued to play football his senior year in high school, but suddenly it was less important than it had once been. His principle changed. His new guiding principle is to become an orthopedic surgeon. If strong enough, this principle will guide him through college, through medical school and make him a successful orthopedic surgeon.

As you make decisions during your career, you will learn to use your principles as a chain of reasoning. You'll apply what's important to you to the situation you're currently facing. Just like Jack changed his principles when something else became more important in his life, you may also find yourself making changes to what you once thought was extremely important.

For example, when you were single, perhaps your job was the most important thing in your life. It drove many of your decisions. Staying late or working a Saturday was probably never an issue. You might have even taken work home because, after all, work was the most important thing to you. It was your principle.

One day you met someone who became very important in your life. Your job was still very important to you, but so was this person. As a result, you started making different decisions about your priorities. You suddenly started realizing life wasn't all about just work. Eventually you married and one day you had a child together. Suddenly your life changed immensely. Your top priority became your family and especially your newborn child. While it was important to keep your job, nothing was more important than your child. Everything you did from the moment of their birth, was done with your child in mind. Your child, and eventually your children, as your family grew, became your top priority and your guiding principle.

When your principles change like this, your chain of reasoning evolves to include these updated criteria. You start making decisions based on work/life balance instead of concentrating on just work or just your family. Both your family and your job are important to you, so now you need to work on making sure they are appropriately balanced. You don't need to abandon a principle entirely in order to adopt a new principle. It just means you now have to assess priority in your decision-making process.

You will use chain of reasoning based upon your principles throughout your life. You'll make decisions based upon how important your principles are at the time. Just remember that while a principle may be important to you today, at any time you may add additional principles or abandon old ones as they become more or less important in your life.

Chapter 15: Rely on Your Values

Values are beliefs that are the foundation of our lives. They are handed down from generation to generation in our families and will probably never change. They will guide us through life and will always be there for us.

Let's say your family has a strong religious belief. Your great-grandparents were strong believers, your grandparents were strong believers, your parents were strong believers and they raised you as a strong believer. You have learned to trust God and to go to him in times of abundance and in times of trouble. Nothing will ever fracture your faith in God. You may stray once in a while, but you will always come back to your strong faith in God and know that he will always be there for you. That value is foundational for you and no matter what path you take through life, you will always have your faith to guide you.

Let's use another example of a value. Let's say your family raised you with a strong awareness of "Family". You remain very close to your mother, your father and your siblings throughout your life. You spend most holidays together. When one of you is going through a tough time, your family is your support group. There isn't anything any member of your family wouldn't do for each other.

Compare that to someone who doesn't have a close family or maybe no family at all. Perhaps they grew up in a broken home or perhaps siblings live far apart and rarely, if ever, get together. Does that mean the person who doesn't share your "Family" value isn't going to be successful? Not in the least. It just means they may have different values than you. They have different values as their foundation, values they can always rely on. Perhaps that person's value is work hard and giving maximum effort to everything they do. If that's the case, that's how they will live their life.

During times of difficulty or stress, we can rely on our values to help us through. Just like a foundation of a building, our values are rock solid and will be there for us even during times of disaster. Since the values of family and faith in God are the easiest to describe, let's use them as examples. When disaster strikes, perhaps a fire, a tornado or a traffic accident, if your value is family, that's who you will turn to for comfort. If your value is faith, you will immediately turn to prayer.

The same holds true for times of abundance. When you receive good news, if your value is family, it's family you call first. You can't wait to share the news with them. If your value is faith in God, you offer prayers of thanksgiving appreciating what God has provided.

Let's say your value is hard work. When you become stressed, oftentimes you will focus and perhaps even increase your efforts at work. Why? Because that is the value upon which you've learned to depend. You will always return to your values in times of doubt.

I once spoke with a man about values who promptly declared he had none. He had no family to which he was close. He believed in God but hadn't spoken to him in a very long time. His job was just a job. He really couldn't think of anything he felt strongly about. I asked him what he did when he really became stressed. He said he went hiking. He said there was nothing like going out into the field, becoming one with nature. There, he said, he could get away from everything and think. His value was nature, or perhaps, hiking.

Values don't have to fit a certain pattern. They are whatever is extremely important to each of us. While our values can be similar with others, they can just as easily be something so unique that no one else shares them. Our intensities, when it comes to values, also vary from person to person. I've known people that have family as a value that can't make a decision without first wanting full family approval. I've known others who don't have to go to that extreme. The important thing about values is they will never change, and they will always be there for us.

Now that you know the difference, you can easily see how perceptions, principles and values help guide our lives. We'll have thousands of perceptions during our life. Some will remain with us and some will disappear almost as quickly as we formed them. Perceptions are adaptable and can be easily changed based upon additional observations. Some will be important, and some will be trivial. I didn't like oysters when I was young. Now I love them. Perhaps I refused to try them because I didn't like the thought of eating something that looked like that.

The typical person will have hundreds of principles during their life. Most of them will be important, at least at the time. Some of them may come and go as life changes and we mature. We'll abandon some and we'll develop some new ones. Principles help guide our life and how we interact with others. They allow us to grow and develop but cut down on the chaos that surrounds us. Principles help us focus on what's important at the time.

Values, on the other hand, will always be there for us and will never change. We'll only have a few values in our life, but they will be extremely important to us. Even if we find ourselves abandoning them at times, they will always be there should we decide to come back. You may go away to college and lose contact with family members, but your family will always be there for you should you need them.

Values are our foundation. They've been handed down through our family for generations. They are our rock. They will get us through life. Most importantly, you'll hand your values on to your children and the same values that guided you through life will guide them through life. That's pretty amazing when you really think about it. Cherish your values. They are the most important gift you will ever, ever receive.

Chapter 16: Work Through Issues

Let's be honest, no job is a walk in the park every single day. Periodically, issues will arise. When they do, don't let them fester. Deal with them. Most issues will involve another person. The first step to clear up any uncertainties or when dealing with any problem involving another person is to talk with them. Although that seems scary, you'll be surprised how well a tactful, heart-felt conversation will help.

If it involves your boss, ask them to sit down with you, but here's the key: be sincere, honest, genuine and heart-felt in your request. Oftentimes, the way you handle your request for a talk will determine how well the talk will go. If it isn't your boss, but someone else you work with, then adapt these concepts accordingly.

I once went through some training about how to approach other people. During that training, the trainer used the analogy of an open window. You are on one side of the window and the other person is on the other. Your goal is to approach this person in such a way that they keep their window open instead of slamming it shut in your face. If you approach your boss telling them you'd really like to work on yourself and need their input, chances are they will be willing to keep their window open and the conversation going. If you approach your boss aggressively or with a chip on your shoulder and give them the impression the conversation will be difficult, chances are their window will slam shut. Think of it this way, your first goal is to keep the conversation going. Everyone loses once the window is shut.

When you're talking with your boss about an issue, be specific and concise. Don't bombard them with anything and everything that's on your mind. Focus on the main issue and explain it in detail. Own it. Acknowledge your participation and perhaps even cause in the issue and be willing to propose ideas that could benefit everyone involved. Be sincere and tactful. Work towards win-win. Listen to any input your boss provides and be open to ideas. Agree on a plan and implement it. Even if the issue doesn't get resolved immediately, stick to the plan and give it time to play out. Meet frequently and discuss progress. Propose modifications. Don't give up. Give it your maximum effort.

What do you do if you've given it your maximum effort and the issue continues? Go back to your boss and try again. If that doesn't help, then it's time to make some tough decisions. You may have to take the issue to someone else, as we'll discuss later, or you may have to evaluate if the issue is of such importance that you would need to take further steps. Don't enter any decision lightly, but don't remain in a job that makes you miserable either.

It's important to remember that not every perception you hold is accurate or true. During your discussion with your boss is the best time to find out and clear up any incorrect perceptions you may be holding. Again, tact is the key if you feel any of these perceptions could put your boss on the defensive. Your goal is not to win the discussion, but rather to assure the discussion occurs. This is also the perfect time to find out if your boss has any perceptions he/she is carrying that may or may not be accurate.

Let's talk about an example. Years ago, I had someone I worked with that I could sense was on edge when we talked. I wasn't her boss, but rather her boss's boss. Regardless, since she worked in my department, I saw her nearly every day in the office. She never said anything specific, but I could just sense something was wrong.

One day I decided to ask her about it. I attempted to do it in the most tactful way as possible because I wanted to keep our window open. I didn't want her to get uncomfortable or defensive. I approached the subject saying, "Rita, sometimes I sense that I make you uncomfortable. What am I doing to make you feel that way?" You'll notice instead of placing the blame on her and asking her why she was uncomfortable, I owned it and tried to give her the impression I was truly interested in working on any problem I may be causing. She didn't respond immediately, but rather just looked at me. I gave her time to gather her thoughts. When she finally spoke, she said, "When I come into the office in the morning, you never say 'Good Morning' or 'Hello', so it makes me think you're mad at me."

Quite honestly, I had never given that much thought. Mornings were usually rather hectic for me. I typically arrived early, before anyone else got there, and I usually dove right into my work as soon as I arrived at the office. I didn't realize not going around and greeting people in the morning when they came in could make anyone feel like I was mad at them. This was going to be an easy fix. From the next morning on, I made sure I went around and said good morning to all of my people as soon as they arrived. Magically, my relationship with Rita began to improve. What seemed insignificant to me was important to her. She had developed a perception based upon her observations and although her conclusion was inaccurate, it was her perception and nothing I could say would change that. The only way I was able to change that perception was by showing her I had listened and modified my behavior. Continuing to ignore her in the morning, would never have changed her perception. I had to physically show her I wasn't mad at her.

During your discussion with your boss, refer to your principles. What's the real issue and why is it affecting you so deeply? What could be done to rectify the situation? What do I need to work on? What do I see as a way that could resolve this that would benefit everyone? Don't assume your boss already knows these things. He/she may have something completely different in mind and have no idea what is really important to you. Use this discussion to assure you both are on the same page and be open to ideas that perhaps you hadn't previously considered.

Rely on your values. When you have your conversation, your values are your safe place. They have guided you through life, will never change and will always be there for you. Even when you've gone astray, your values will welcome you back. Think of them as your armor. They will protect you and woe to any person that attempts to make you violate them without your permission. During your discussion with your boss, you probably will change some of your perceptions. You may even modify or add to your principles, but never be flexible when it comes to your values. They are the most important thing you will ever own.

We've all worked for people that we've liked and some that we haven't liked. We learned from each of them and hopefully you came away a better person because of them. Perhaps you've picked up some of the traits or adopted some of the successful techniques of your good bosses. Hopefully you've learned what not to do and techniques to avoid from your poor bosses. It's important that we learn from both. We develop our leadership style based upon the things we've learned and decided to adopt from others.

The good boss is easy. You get along well. You can go to them for help. They are attentive to your needs. Life is pretty good when you have a good boss.

Life isn't so good with a difficult boss. You've had The Talk and you've attempted to hit the reset button with them several times, to no avail. What do you do? I'm a firm believer that you never go over your boss's head with a problem or concern until you've first attempted to discuss it one-on-one with them. In some cases, your boss may not even realize there is a problem. It's only fair to discuss the problem with them and give them an opportunity to correct it. If they are unwilling or unable to work on it, then that's another story and you have an obligation to yourself to take the issue up the ladder.

I once had a boss that, for some reason, we just didn't click. I would try to do the best job I could for them, but I never received acknowledgement for anything I did. If I happened to make any mistakes, he was on me in a minute, but if I did something right, I never heard a word from him. Our management styles were completely different. That happens in companies and you just have to learn to work through them. In such cases, you have to remain true to yourself and honor your principles but remain open enough to learn new methods and techniques that your boss may utilize or propose.

I'm a huge believer in relationships. It's how I've always managed. My new boss was very much a loner. He didn't like dealing with people. He would prefer not to talk to people, but instead gather their data, assemble it and draw his own conclusions. I prefer to get everyone in a room and have an open discussion. He preferred to use the conclusions he had drawn, make a decision and send it out in an email to all of his direct reports. It was obvious our relationship was going to be challenging. I attempted to keep an open mind and do the best job I could providing him what he needed.

At a certain point, after numerous challenges, I asked to have a heart-to-heart talk with him. He agreed to schedule a date and time and then proceeded to postpone it several times. It was obvious he was not looking forward to our discussion. I continued to press, and we eventually met. I used my notes to make sure all relevant topics were covered. I did my best to own any difficulties and to avoid assessing blame, but still get my concerns on the table. At the end of the meeting, we both agreed to hit the reset button and make our reporting relationship work.

Long story short, I had this same reset discussion with him on three different occasions. The last time, I informed him that either some changes would need to be made or I was going to have to make some decisions. Those decisions would include options of 1) we get on the same page; 2) I push my concerns up the ladder; or 3) me leaving the company. I'm sure he was hoping for the later, but I first felt I owed it to the company to try one more time. This attempt also ultimately failed.

After careful consideration, I felt I needed to go to a higher level. I wasn't trying to throw him under the bus, but someone needed to know some of the things that were going on. I contacted our Human Resources Department and scheduled a meeting with one of the HR representatives. During that discussion, I didn't try to paint my boss in a bad light; I simply gave them some examples of what was happening, and I spoke from my heart. It was obvious some of what had happened was not in the best interest of the company.

My boss ended up getting fired. I later learned I was not the only one having problems with him. Several of my peers were having the same problems I was experiencing, and I learned he wasn't meeting the expectations of upper management. My call to HR was simply one more reason that his employment needed to be evaluated. I don't take delight in the fact he was terminated; I took it as a failure on my part. I wish there was something I could have done to help him. The only solace I had was knowing that I had tried on several occasions to sit down with him and talk.

Why am I sharing this with you? Because at some point in your career, you're going to be faced with a similar situation. You're going to have a boss with whom you have difficulty getting along. I strongly, strongly encourage you to make every attempt to work through your problems one-on-one with your boss and attempt it on multiple occasions, if that's what is needed. Only then can you feel comfortable that you did everything you could to help them. If all of your attempts fail, you have options. I would encourage you to talk to HR or take it to your boss's boss, but make sure you've given your boss plenty of opportunities to discuss and work on the problems first. If going higher up doesn't work, you still have the option to leave the company. Sometimes you have to make those tough choices. Sometimes it's just not a perfect fit. You have an obligation to look out for your best interests and you have a right to exercise any ethical option. Just make sure you rely on your values and principles when you choose one of these options. Don't rely on your perceptions; perceptions can often be wrong.

Chapter 17: Integrity

There are tons of quotes available on integrity and a lot of them are really good. I prefer to use the following composite of them all, but one that means a lot to me.

The only thing a person will ever truly own is their integrity.

Why do I feel so passionate about integrity? It's because integrity is what makes a person trustworthy and without trust, there can be no relationship.

Let's dive into that a bit further. Having integrity doesn't mean just saying what is honest. It also means doing what you say you are going to do. If I lie to you, I'm not being honest. If I tell you I'm going to do something and then don't do it, I've in effect lied to you and no relationship will survive on lies. You need to be able to trust what I'm telling you is truthful and honest. You need to be able to rely on me that I will follow through on what I've told you I will do.

There's one other kind of lie that can greatly affect your integrity. That's the lie of omission. Has anyone ever led you to believe something, but perhaps while telling you, they left out some of the important details? Perhaps the details they just happened to leave out were the details that involved them. When you approached them on it, their response was "I didn't lie; I just didn't tell you the whole story." That's a lie of omission.

It's easy to get caught up in a lie of omission because it's human nature not to want to deliver bad news, so we sugar-coat things or make it seem likes it's trivial when really the issue is something quite important. Have you ever taken action on something someone told you only to find out later you didn't have all the facts or that the facts you had weren't quite accurate or complete? We all have, and we've all been guilty of leaving out important facts to protect ourselves or someone else. The problem with lies of omissions is you can't properly deal with a problem unless you have the facts and, in most cases, all of the facts. Withholding details often results in improper action being taken, innocent people being accused, hard feelings and a loss of integrity. To avoid lies of omissions, share what you factually know to be true and own any involvement you may have had in the process.

Think about the symbiotic organisms that rely on integrity. Certainly, in mutualism, both organisms need to be able to trust and rely on each other. In a commensalism relationship, only one of the organism's benefits, so no trust really ever develops between them. The host is being used by the other organism. Certainly, there is no trust in a predation type of relationship. In parasitism, the parasite will eventually harm or kill the host, so no trust there. Competition, however, is a little different. There's a lot of trust in a healthy competition type of relationship, but no trust at all in an unhealthy type of competition.

Integrity applies to all you do in life, but we're going to just talk about its effect on your work life. During the course of your career, I'm sure you've worked with or run across someone who lacks integrity. Perhaps you've caught them in a lie or perhaps they didn't follow through on things they promised to do. How did you react to that person? After being burned a few times, my guess is you avoided that person like the plague. Since you couldn't trust them, you didn't care to be around them. The opposite holds true for someone who displays integrity. You probably enjoy being around them and would gladly work with them on a project because you know you can trust their honesty and their honoring of commitments.

Now look at your own life at work. Are you the person everyone can trust? If not, why not? Are you the person that always honors your commitment? If not, why not? If you answered no to either question, the time to fix that is today. If you're going to become the best you can be, you have to commit to being the best person you can be and that starts with integrity. So, how do you fix it? The first thing you need to do is have a one-on-one heartfelt talk with anyone to whom you may not have shown integrity. Approach that person, speak from your heart, own the fact that you haven't always been a person of integrity in the past, but then let them know you see that now and you're really going to work on correcting it. If you are honest, sincere and truly speak from your heart, you probably at least got the window cracked to perhaps continue the conversation, but remember, this person may have a perception of you that words won't fix. You have to show them that you are different than their original perception. You have to show them you are really trying.

If you answered yes to all the original questions, then just keep up the great work. Remember, once in a while you'll slip up. Something may prevent you from keeping a commitment, but when that happens, own it, speak from your heart with that person and your integrity will remain intact.

Stephen Covey, in his book Seven Habits of Highly Effective People talks about relationships using the analogy of a bank account. As you establish trust with another person, it's like making a deposit into their emotional bank account. The more nice things you do for them, the more deposits you make and the higher the balance in their emotional bank account goes. A day may come, however, when you need a favor or have some bad news you need to share with them and have to make a withdrawal from their emotional bank account. As long as you had a large enough balance in their account before the withdrawal, it will probably go smoothly, but if you don't have a large enough balance, you take the risk of overdrawing the account and will need to suffer the consequences. The lesson to be learned is to make deposits in everyone's emotional bank account and you'll never have to worry about the rare withdrawals.

When you're dealing with your boss, integrity is key. They have to be able to rely on you. They have to trust that assignments will be completed as promised. They have to know you are honest with them. When you mess up, own it. Go to them first and report it. Don't let your boss get blind-sided when the problem finally rears its ugly head. Apologize and then be ready to present a plan for not only fixing it, but to prevent it from happening again in the future.

I've messed up plenty of times in my career. I've made a lot of mistakes. One of my proudest moments, however, was when my boss told me how proud he was of me that I always owned my mistakes and was always willing to work to assure they never happened again. I have a feeling that relieved some anxiety for my boss. He had several people reporting to him and sometimes he heard about mistakes after it was too late to fix them, but he could always count on me to keep him informed and do what I needed to do to correct any deficiencies. As for mistakes, they're going to happen. It's how we learn. If we live in a safe world and never take chances, we'll never grow. If you make a mistake, learn from it. Don't let the opportunity to learn slip from your grip.

That's how you build integrity with your boss. Mutualistic relationships are built on integrity.

Chapter 18: Respect

Respect is a key component in any relationship. As humans, we develop respect for a person and that respect often lies deep in our hearts. We may never tell them, but it's there and it will show in the way we treat them. In fact, it's easy to treat someone well when we respect them, but what happens when you haven't yet developed respect for a person, or they've done something that prevents us from respecting them?

I've always believed there are actually two types of respect. There is the respect you have for someone that has earned it and there is respect you have for someone because of position. By position, I'm not necessarily referring to status, although status may play a role. It can simply mean I respect someone or something because they are a creature of God and deserve to be treated properly. When I walk down the street and see someone I don't know, I may nod or even say, "Good morning." I may not know who that person is or what that person is like, but I've respected them. I didn't prejudge them for the way they looked or the clothes they were wearing. I simply gave them respect as a creature of God's making.

When I was working for a large company, infrequently I would run into the owner and CEO. I didn't really know him as a person, but I had respect for what he had accomplished and the fact that he gave me a job. Remember the boss I didn't always get along with? I still respected him as a creature of God and respected the position he was in. As a result, I always tried to treat him properly. Even when I had to go over his head, I did so with respect. The same holds true for people in authority. I may not like everything the President of the United States or a member of Congress does, but I respect them for their position.

Everyone deserves to be treated with respect as a creature of God. Not everyone deserves to hold a place of respect in your heart. See the difference? Everyone deserves to be treated fairly and respectfully. Not everyone deserves to be cherished and treated with the love and affection you reserve for that person who has earned a place of respect in your heart. But let me be clear, that doesn't give you the right to treat anyone poorly.

There's an old saying, a take-off of the golden rule that goes, "Treat others the way you'd like to be treated." I always thought that was good advice until one day when a good friend of mine made me see it differently. She said, "Treat others the way they'd like to be treated." That made me do a lot of thinking. Just because I like to be treated a certain way doesn't necessarily mean someone else does.

I've always enjoyed it when my boss gave me a pat on the back when I did a good job; I mean a physical pat on the back. To me, it meant he was proud of me for what I had accomplished. I began to use that technique when conveying my appreciation to others for a job well done. Several years ago, I gave a pat on the back to one of my people for doing a good job. He actually attempted to dodge it and then turned extremely red in the face. I could tell I had made him extremely uncomfortable. I learned he was the type of person that didn't like to be touched by anyone. In his case, he preferred a kind private comment when no one else was around. I learned from that.

Why are we talking about respect? Because without respect for everyone, you will never be able to establish mutualistic relationships where you work. Understanding the level of respect, however, is key. You may have a boss or a co-worker that has earned your respect and you would do anything for that person. You may also have a boss or a co-worker that you don't really care for. They still deserve to be treated with respect for their position and as a creature of God. You may not care to be around them, and you may not let them into your inner circle of friends, but they still deserve to be treated fairly and humanely.

While we're talking about bosses, let me share one more thought with you. It's often easy to develop perceptions about your boss that may or may not be true. Perhaps we developed that perception based on our observation, but we really didn't know the entire story behind it.

A good example is the time I had someone (Linda) working on our team that was going through some very rough personal problems. I was the leader of the team and although Linda shared her story with me, it was important to her that no one else in the department found out, so I was very careful to keep it extremely quiet. Each day she would come into work looking more stressed and more tired. I suggested the EAP (Employee Assistance Program) and she contacted them for counseling. Her appointment with the EAP was scheduled for an afternoon that week, which just happened to be a rather busy week. When she left in the middle of day for her appointment, a co-worker remarked how this person was allowed to take off in the middle of the day. I couldn't betray Linda's trust and tell the co-worker where she was really going, so I simply didn't respond. The co-worker wasn't especially satisfied with my lack of a response, in fact her comment was, "why is she allowed to schedule an appointment in the middle of the day during a busy time?" She felt I was playing favoritism and allowing special privileges.

Several weeks later, after Linda's life had finally gotten back on the right track, Linda shared her story with her co-workers. The co-worker who had made the remark came up to me and said she was sorry. She didn't know Linda was going through such a tough time and she appreciated the fact that I allowed Linda the time to get some help. She said she also appreciated that I had honored Linda's request to keep her situation private.

Don't let your perceptions result in accusations. If you're concerned about something, talk it out with your boss or co-worker. There may be a good reason why they are doing what they are doing, and they may not be able to completely discuss it with you. Don't allow your perceptions to unjustly distort your behavior. Talking is always better than assuming. Your boss will make mistakes; they're only human. Respect includes forgiveness.

If you're going to become the best you can be, respect and treating people properly has to be part of the equation.

Chapter 19: The Right Team Member

In the previous chapters, we talked a lot about what you can do to change your perception about work, what you can do to make yourself promotable and marketable, and we discussed symbiotic relationships and how relationships with bosses and co-workers are the key to your career path. We talked about The Right Company. Now we're going to talk about The Right Team Member. That's you. No matter what your job is in a company, whether you're the lowest person on the totem pole or the owner of the company, everything we've discussed applies to you.

What can you do to make yourself The Right Team Member? You're already headed down that path by reading this book. By taking the time to read, understand the ideas and work on the concepts, you've demonstrated your willingness to improve; to become the best you can be.

As we've discussed numerous times, relationships at work play a huge role in how you work with and are perceived by others. If you use your talents, give your maximum effort, maintain your integrity, respect others and really work towards mutualistic relationships with everyone you work with, you'll quickly become an up and comer in your organization. Since you strive to share the benefits of your relationships with others, others will be more accepting and actually want to work with you. Although you may introduce healthy competition once in a while, they'll realize they don't have to fear you slipping into predation. They'll understand you're as interested in their benefit as much as you are in yours. Who doesn't want to work around someone like that? In fact, your efforts will be contagious. Others will want to be more like you. And, because you make it a habit to give maximum effort, your boss and other executives in your company will take notice. You'll make connections with people inside and outside your organization and they'll take notice of your maximum effort attitude. The next time they need someone to help them on a project, guess who they will think about? In time, some of the people you work with will be promoted or may even leave the company, but they won't forget about you: the person who gets the most out of every relationship and always gives maximum effort. Don't be surprised if you find yourself being highly recruited. After all, you deserve it.

Being the Right Team Member doesn't mean brown nosing or sucking up to the right people. It doesn't mean being an expert on every subject. It doesn't mean having more talent than anyone else. It means treating people properly, working on relationships, giving maximum effort, setting and adhering to strong principles and always relying on your values. It's not always going to be easy, but I can assure you if you make all of these things a habit, they will come naturally, and you will be The Right Team Member.

Chapter 20: Summing It All Up

Hopefully this book provided you with some insight on how to make your job more fulfilling and enjoyable. If you practice the techniques, you will enhance your career and your life.

There's no reason to see work as a drudgery and, if you do, you can do something about it. Grow your relationships, improve yourself, give maximum effort, rely on your values, be a person of integrity and respect everyone you meet. Those are the secrets to making your work life more fulfilling. We spend a large portion of our lives at work. We might as well get the most out of it. Turning these secrets into habits will not only change your life at work but will benefit all aspects of your life.

So, what's in it for you? When you're able to view relationships as symbiotic, you begin to see relationships in a completely different light. You realize by helping others, you're also helping yourself. Just as importantly, by taking advantage of or hurting others, you're only hurting yourself. Orca's don't last long in the business world. In business, all predators eventually go down in defeat. No one wants to be around them or work with them. When you learn to recognize the symbiotic relationships that are unhealthy, namely: commensalism, predation, parasitism and unhealthy competition, you not only avoid acting in that manner, but you also learn to avoid being around people who behave that way towards others. Once you've found this secret, suddenly the people in your life start to mean more to you. You begin to truly value relationships and cherish those around you.

When working toward becoming the best you can be, suddenly each and every task, each and every project, becomes exciting and worthwhile. It's no longer about just completing a task, but rather improving the task and making it better. As you practice maximum effort, you increase your endurance and the things you're able to accomplish. You experience satisfaction in knowing you've completed a job well done. You leave every task you perform better than it was before and instead of worry or depression from all the things you have yet to accomplish, you begin looking at them as opportunities to make life even better for yourself and for others. When maximum effort becomes a habit, people start noticing. They enjoy working with you and want you on their team. That opens up opportunities and advancement. You become the rising star that companies are eager to hire and promote. The drudgery of going to work in the morning disappears and the excitement of new opportunities becomes real.

You never know when opportunities are going to arise, but if you've prepared yourself properly by making maximum effort a habit and consistently do the best you can do, you'll be ready for them. You will be the person everyone thinks about when deciding who should be promoted or who should be selected to work on a project. Do the best with what you have, because if you've applied maximum effort, it will be enough. You'll make mistakes, but if you learn from them, you haven't failed. An attempt only becomes a failure if you don't allow yourself to learn from it. Apply what you've learned and try again and again until you get it right. Thomas Edison once said, "Many of life's failures are people who did not realize how close they were to success."

It's up to you now. Do you really want to be in the same job 20 or 30 years from now? You have so much more ability than you realize. Invest in yourself. Invest in those around you. You'll quickly see the rewards.

Be good at being you.

So, what are you waiting for? Your career is right in front of you. Go get it!

Don't miss out!

Go to the website below and you can sign up to receive emails whenever Greg Olsen publishes a new book. There's no charge and no obligation.

https://books2read.com/r/B-A-ASMN-OICMB

www.ingramcontent.com/pod-product-compliance
Lightning Source LLC
LaVergne TN
LVHW010627100826
845148LV00014B/3145

9781734333152